This Beautiful Birds Coloring Book Belongs To.

COLOR TEST PAGE

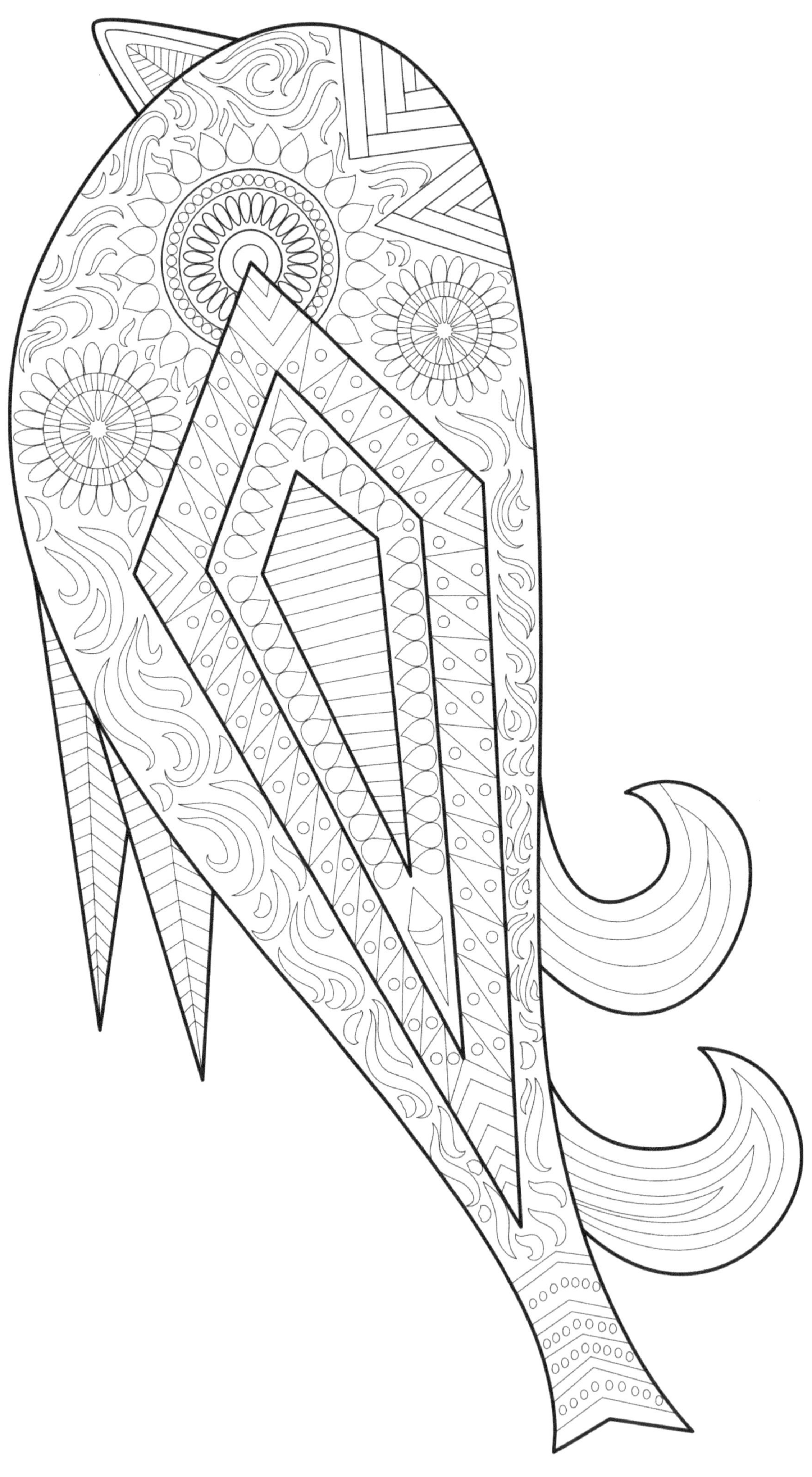

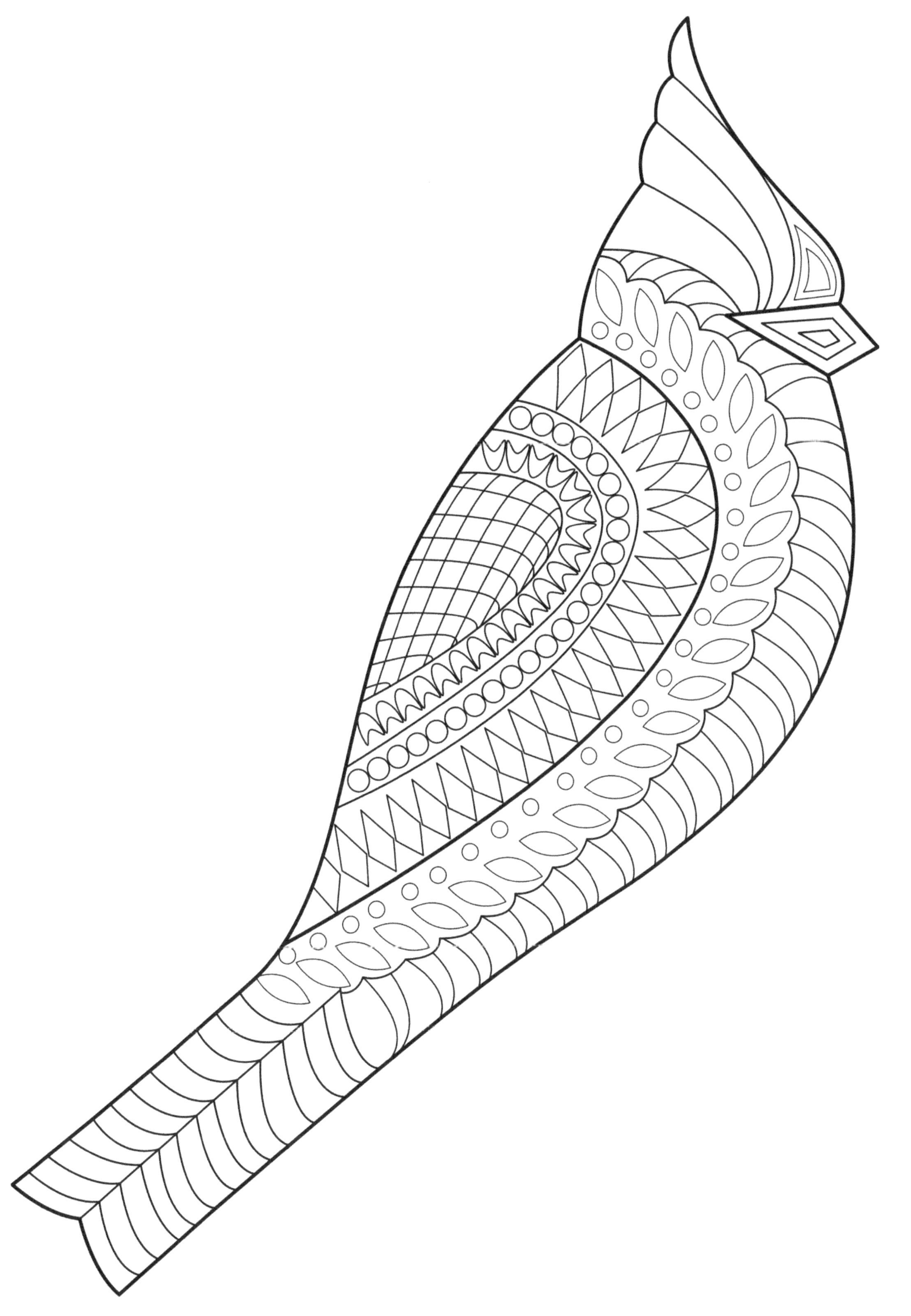

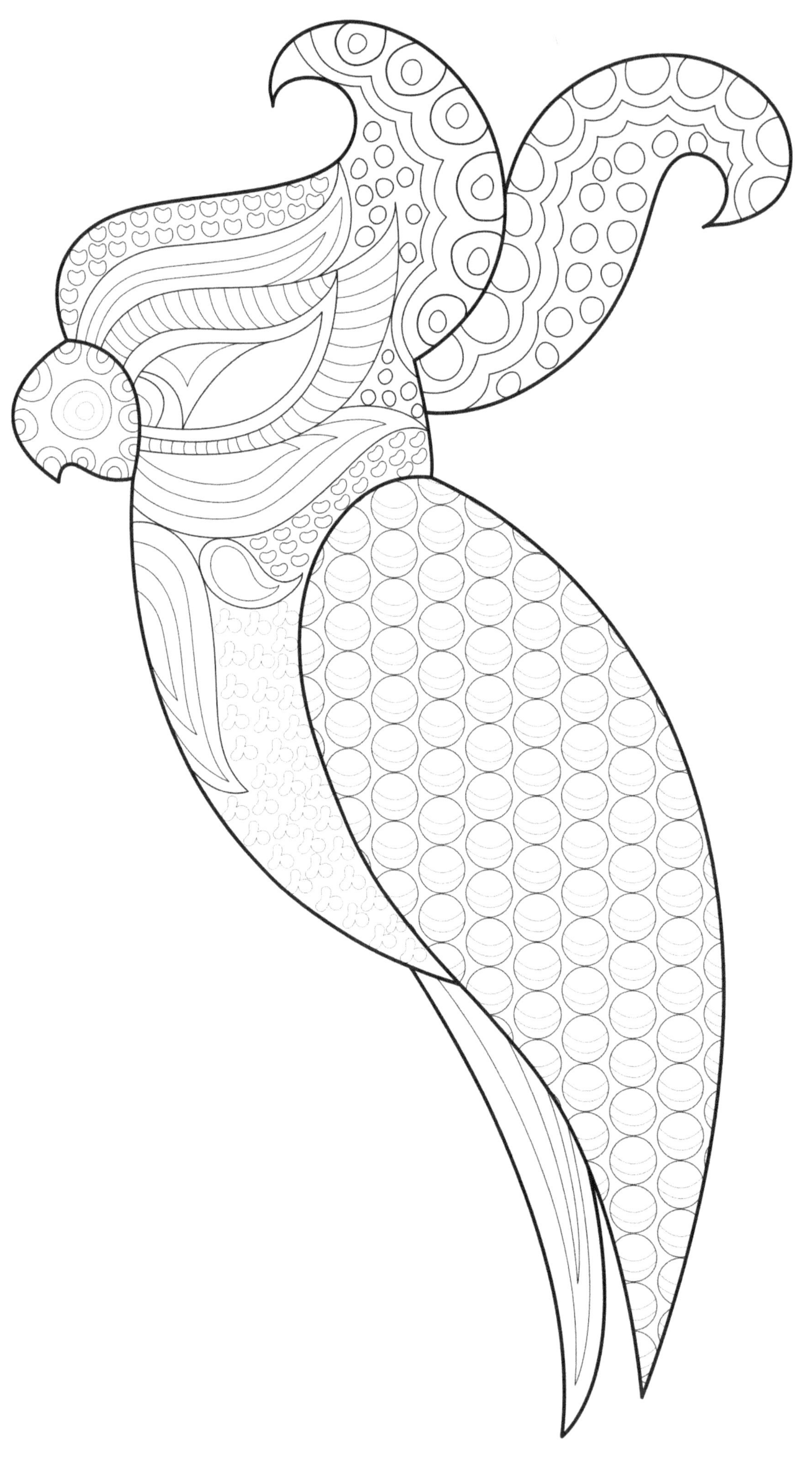

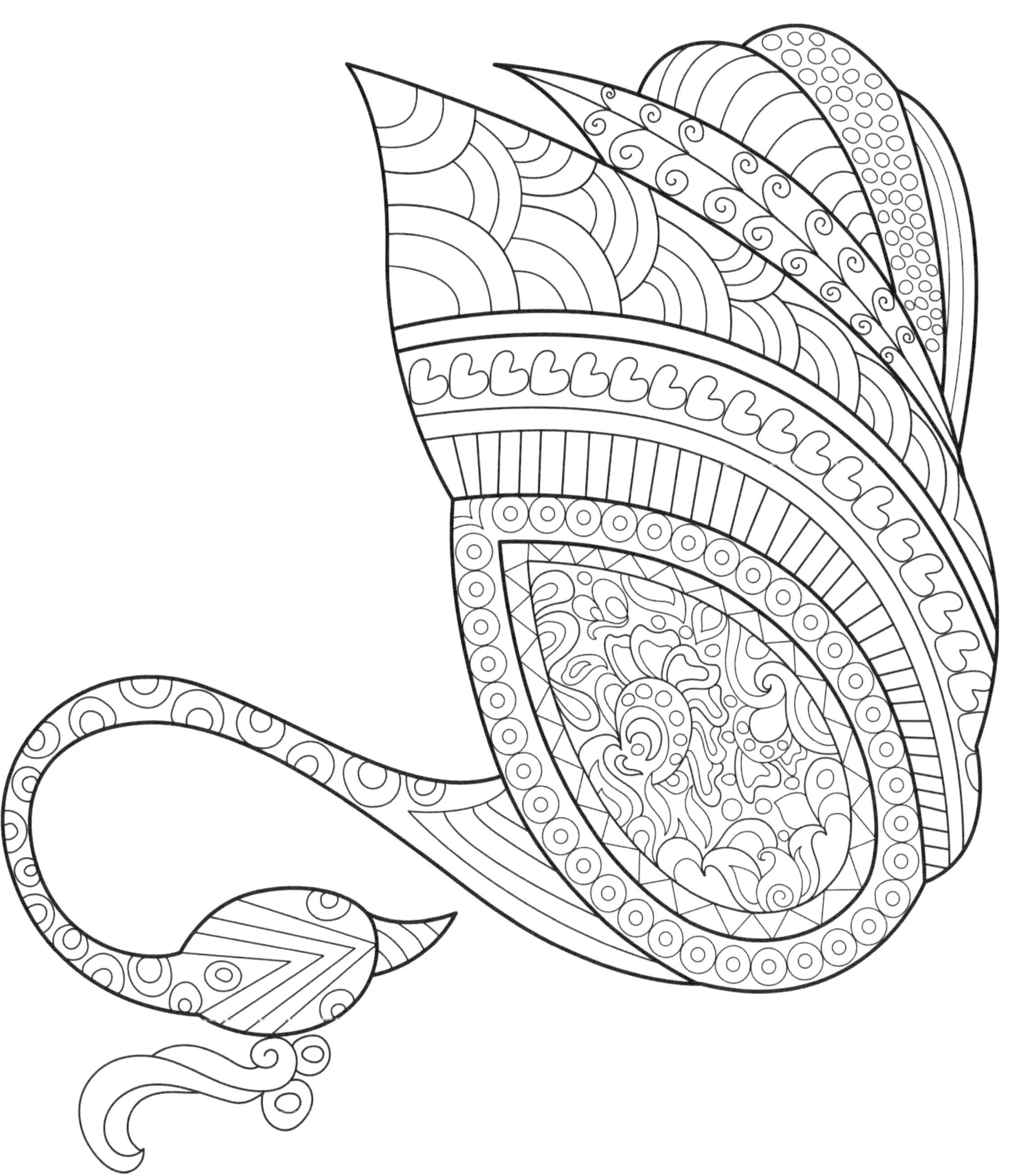

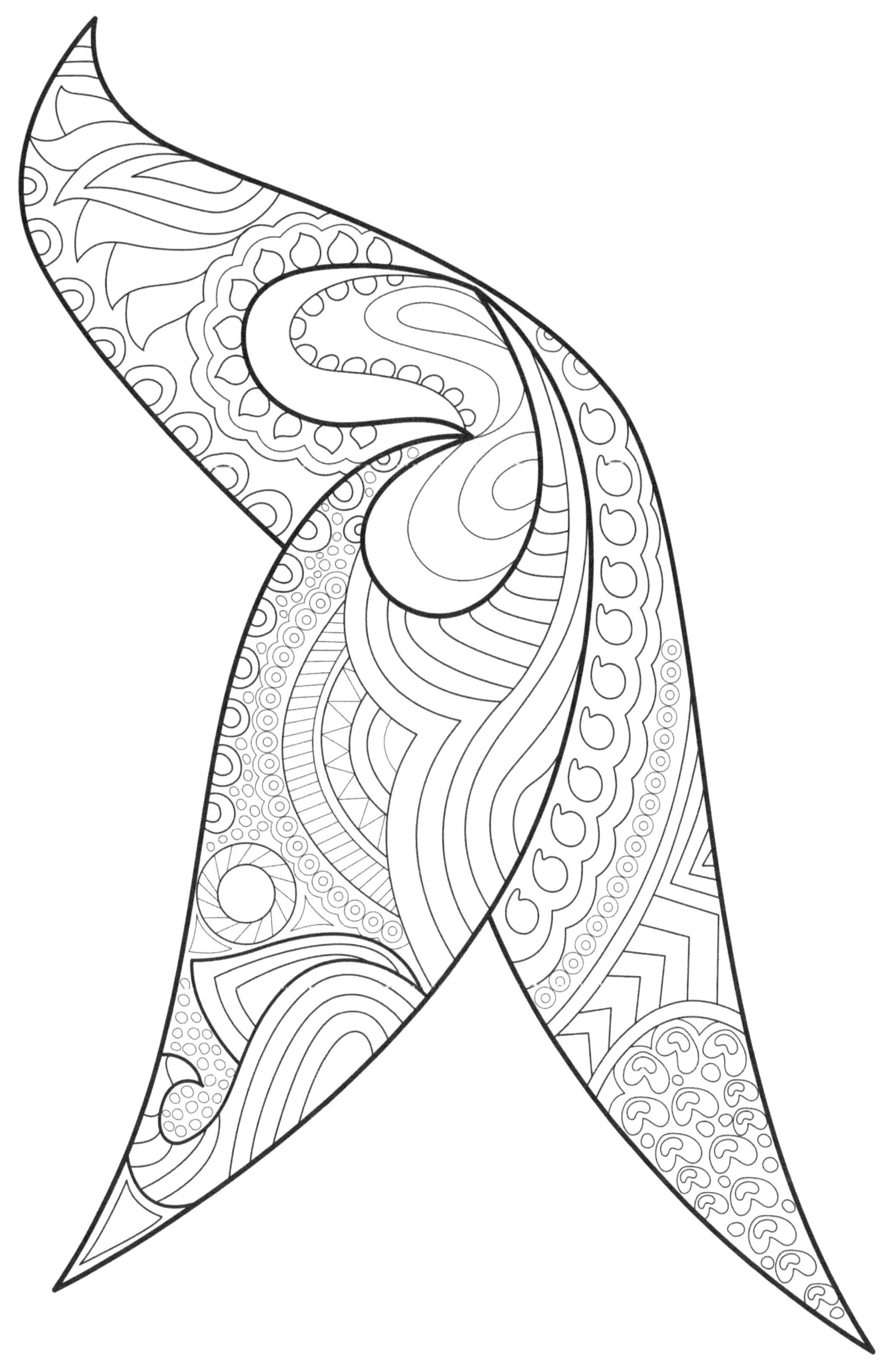

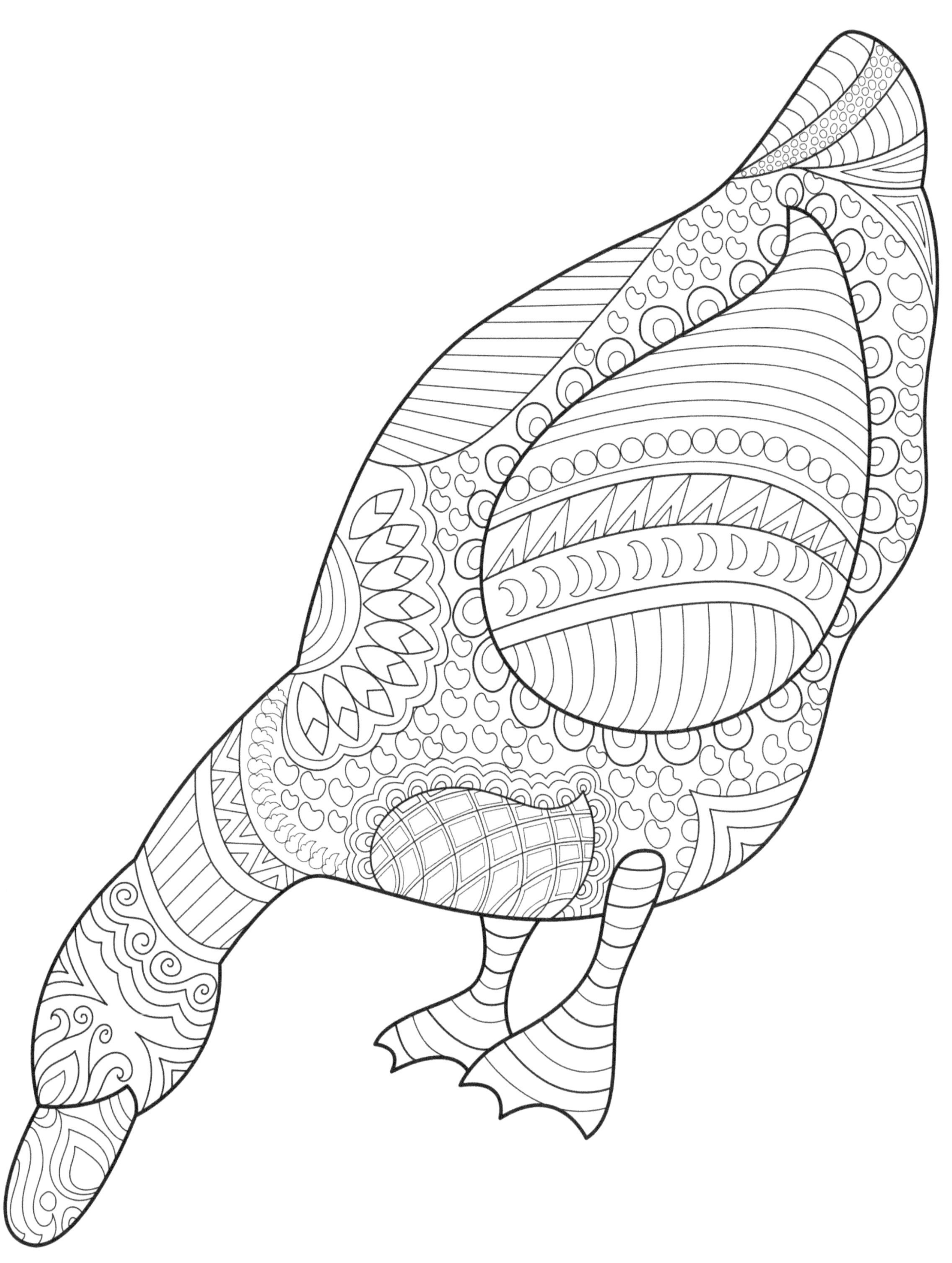

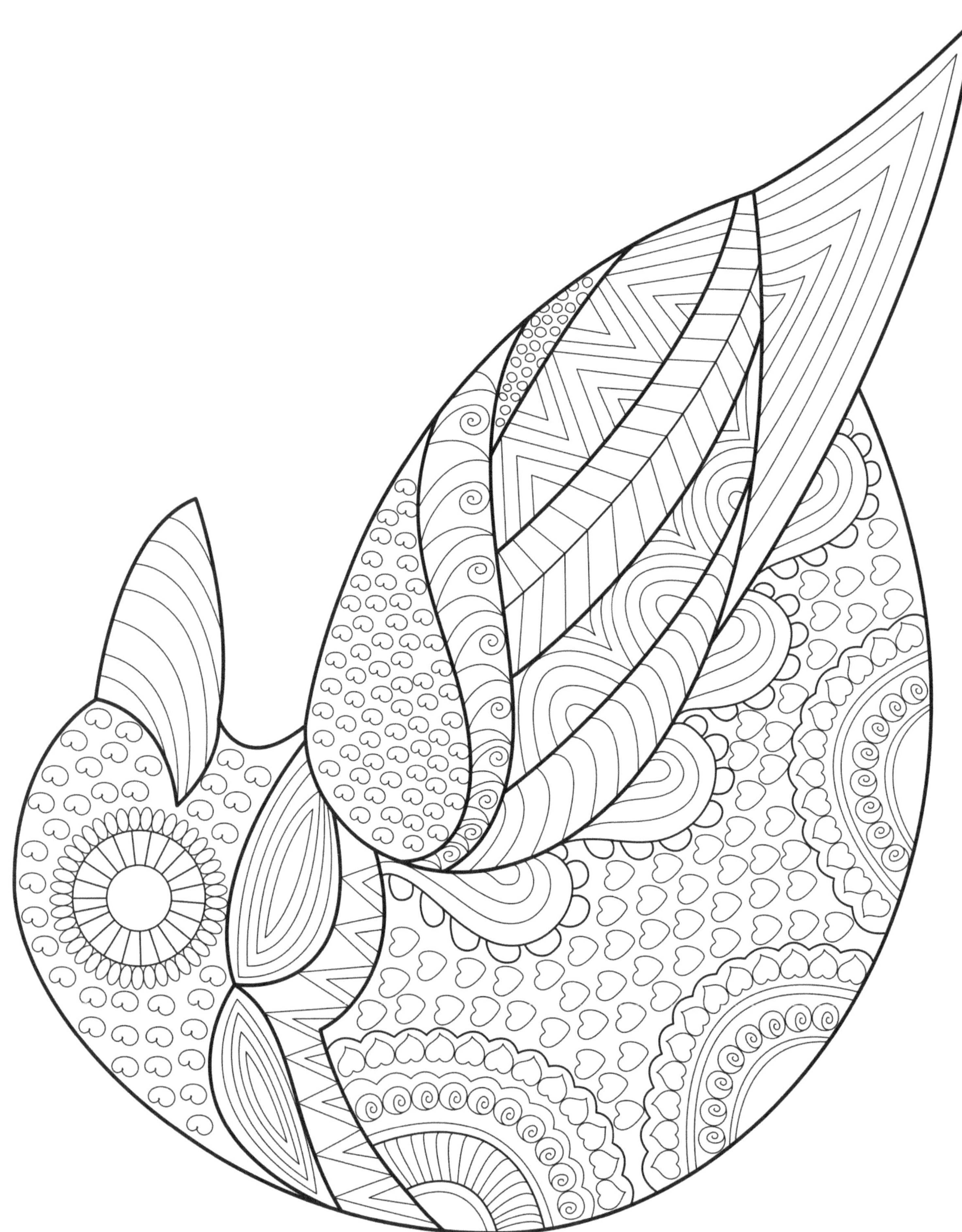

Bored? Solve this Maze

We hope you enjoyed this coloring book, you can find more books on our Store.